CRIMSON CREATURES

A  COLORING BOOK

ABOUT THIS BOOK

Thanks for buying 'Crimson Creatures: A Crimson City Coloring Book'!

Within the pages of this book, you will find a range of detailed creatures for you to discover and color however you like!

For more of my work, please visit www.crimsoncityinc.com or for more coloring books, check out 'Crimson City Inc. A Futuristic Coloring Book'.

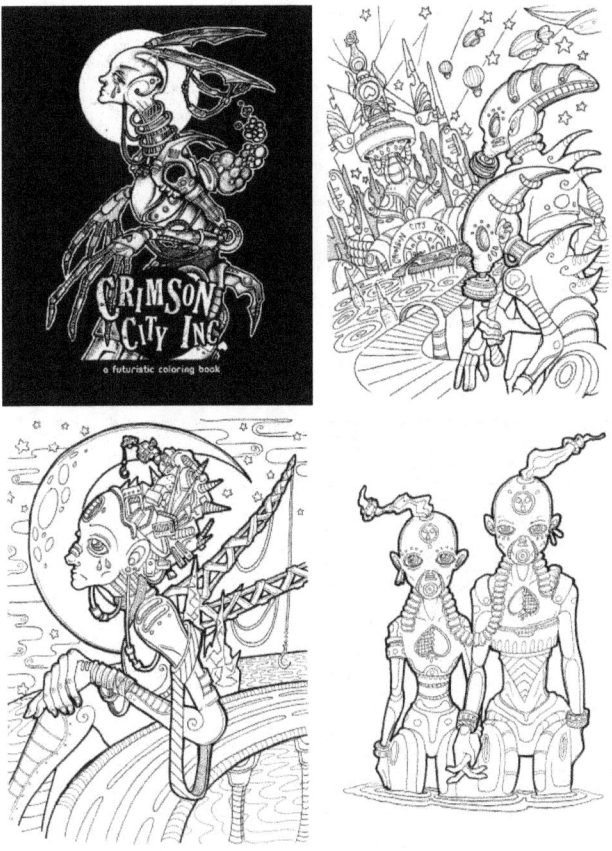

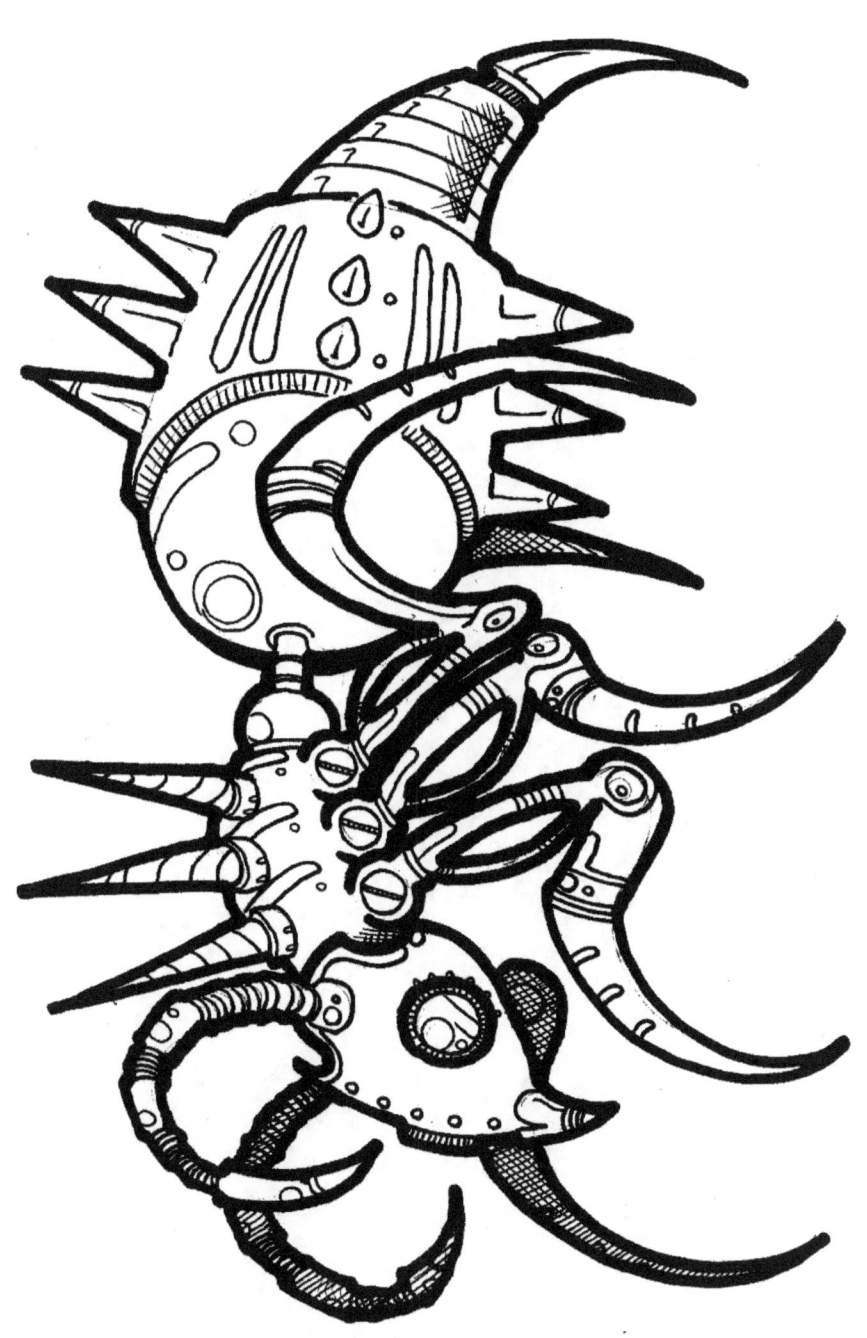

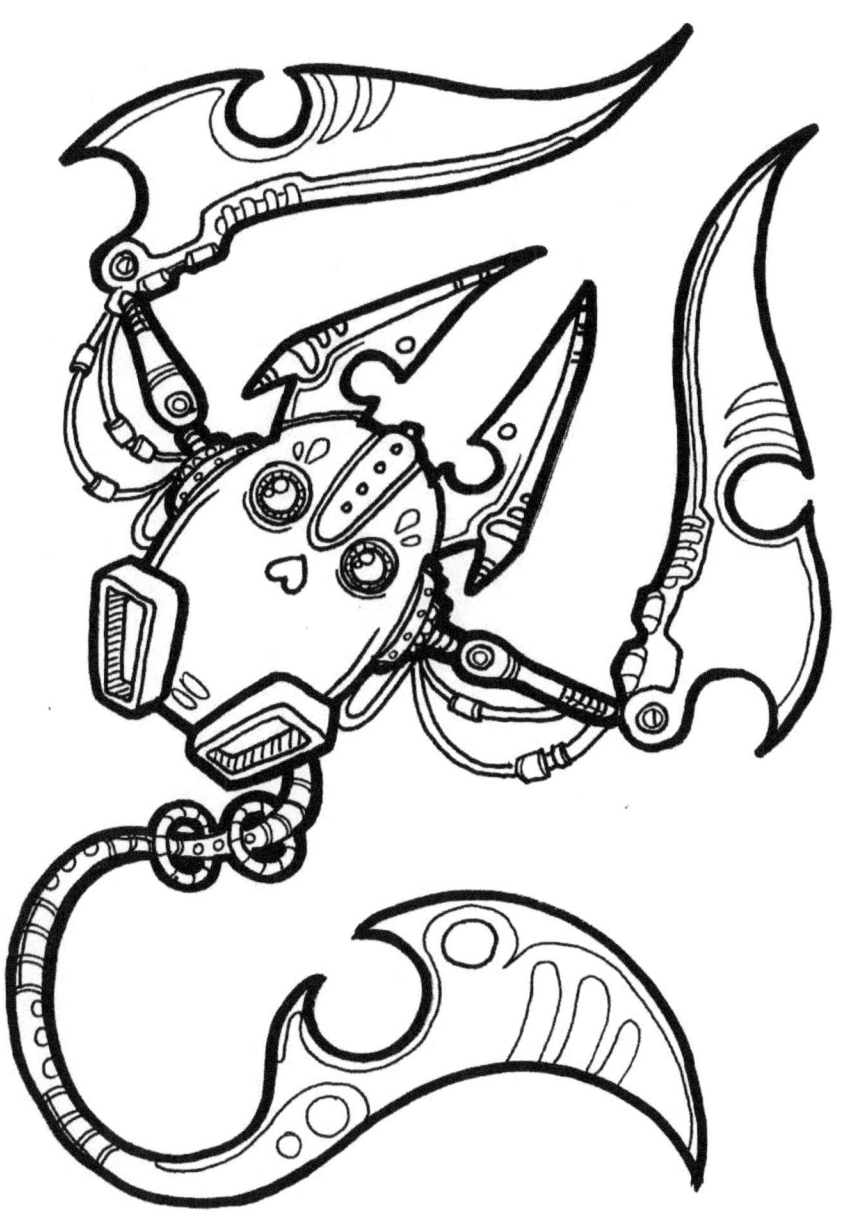

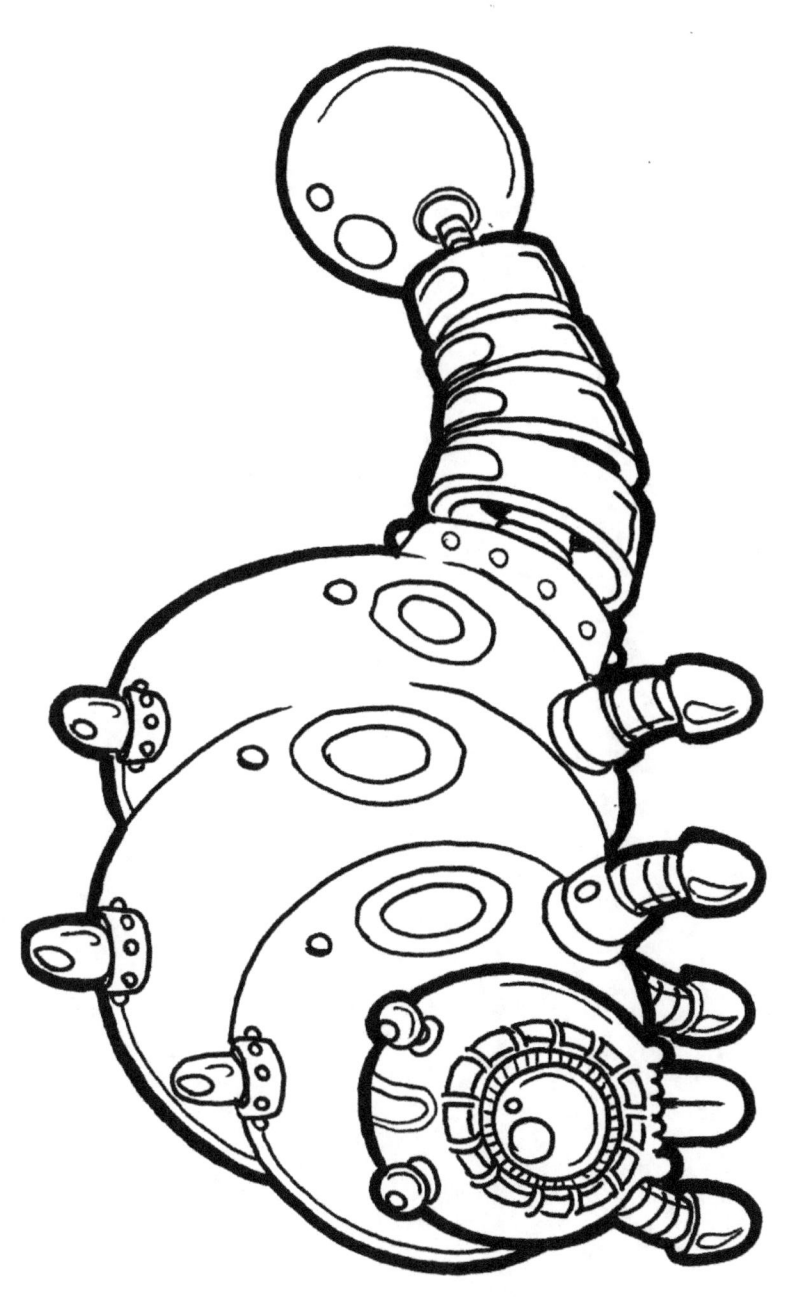

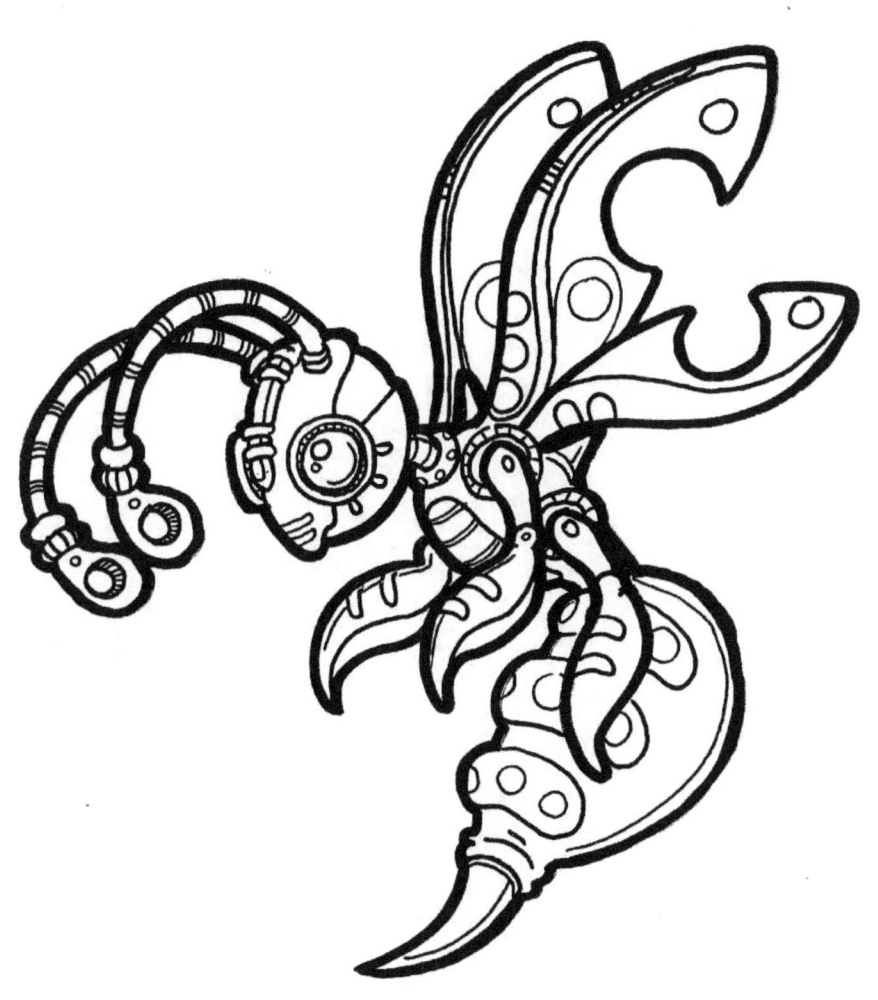

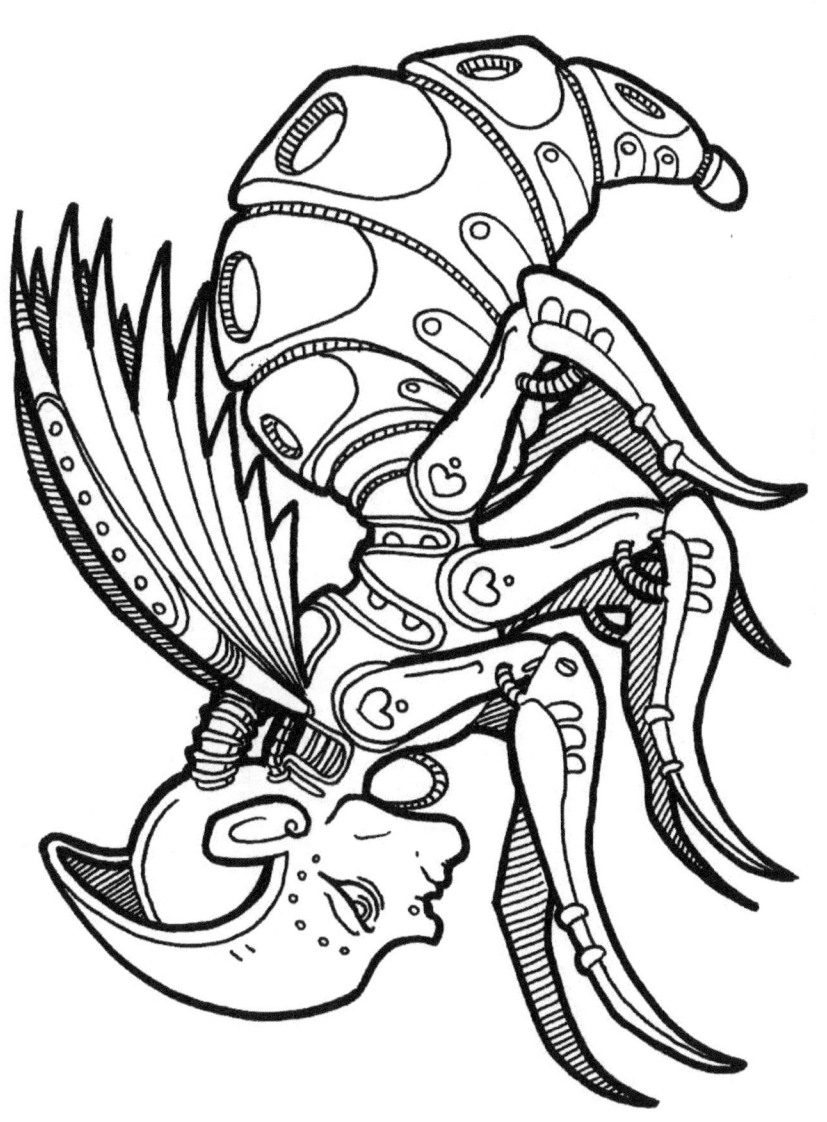

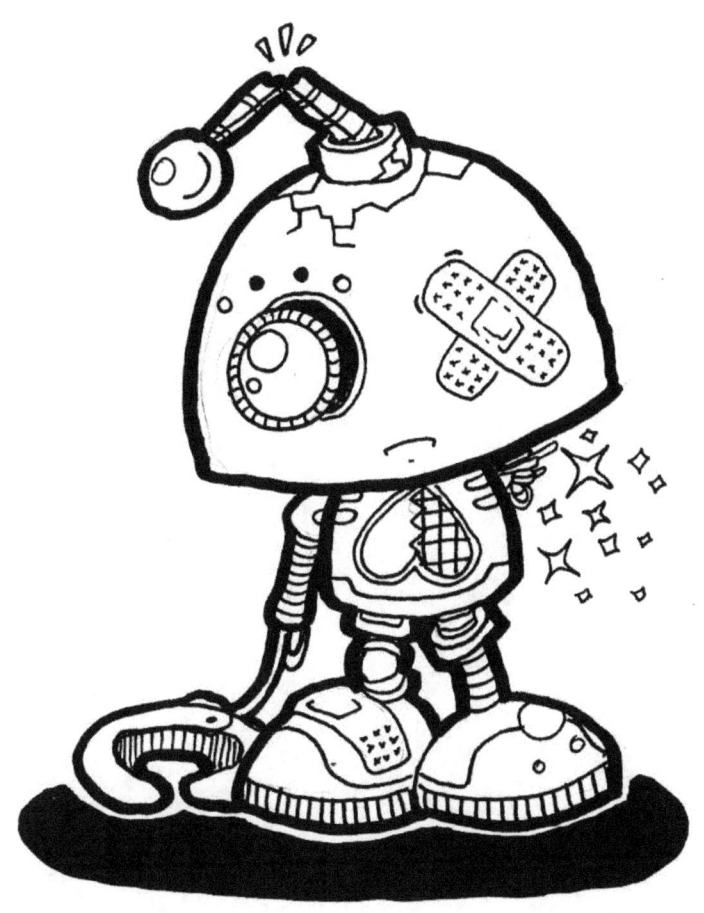

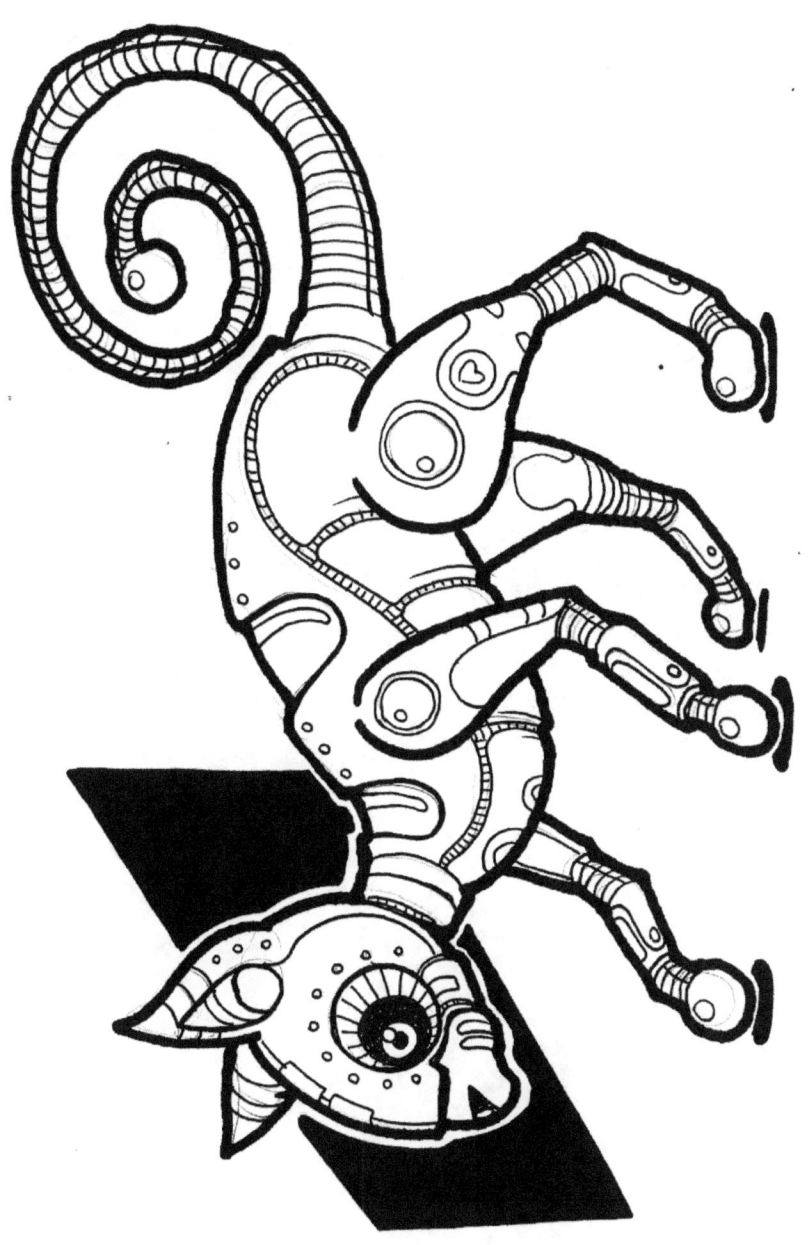

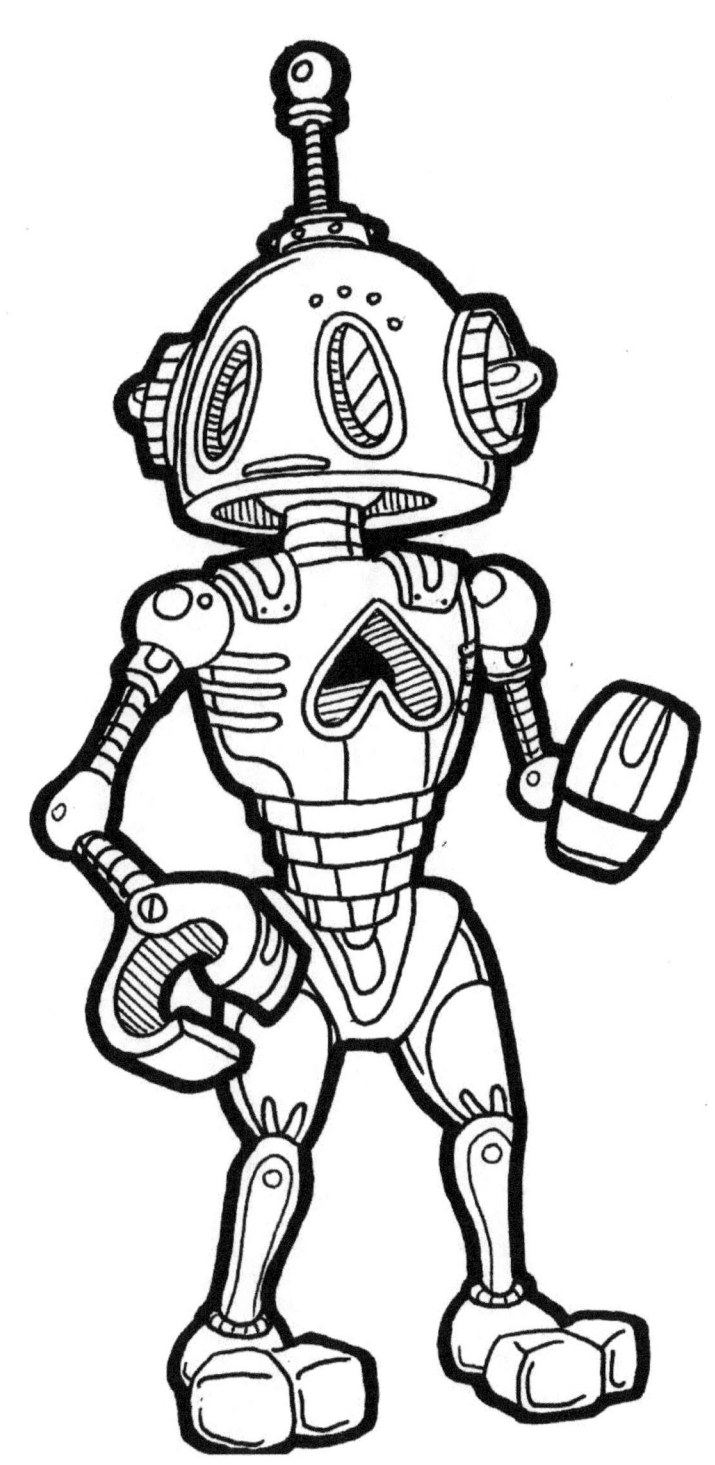

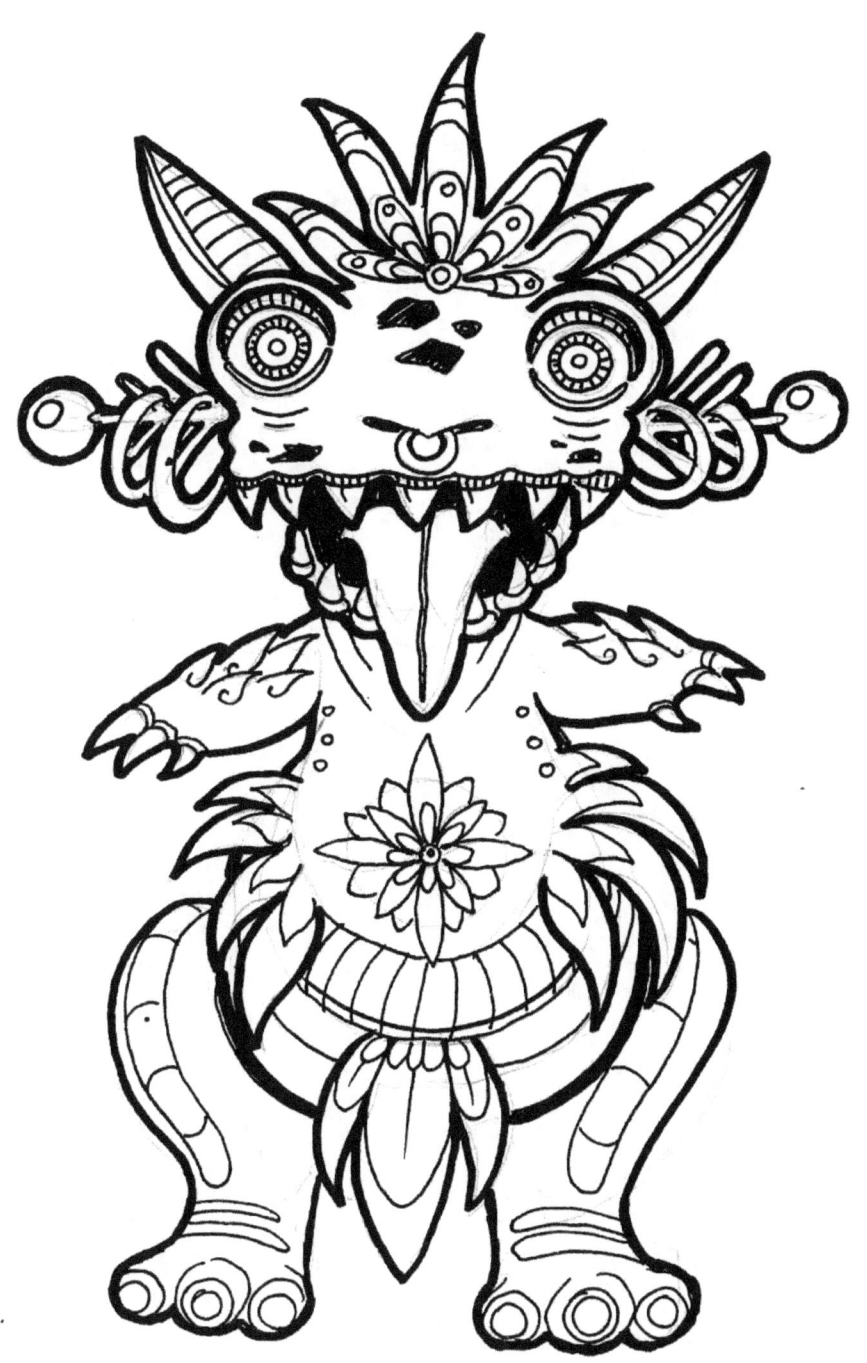

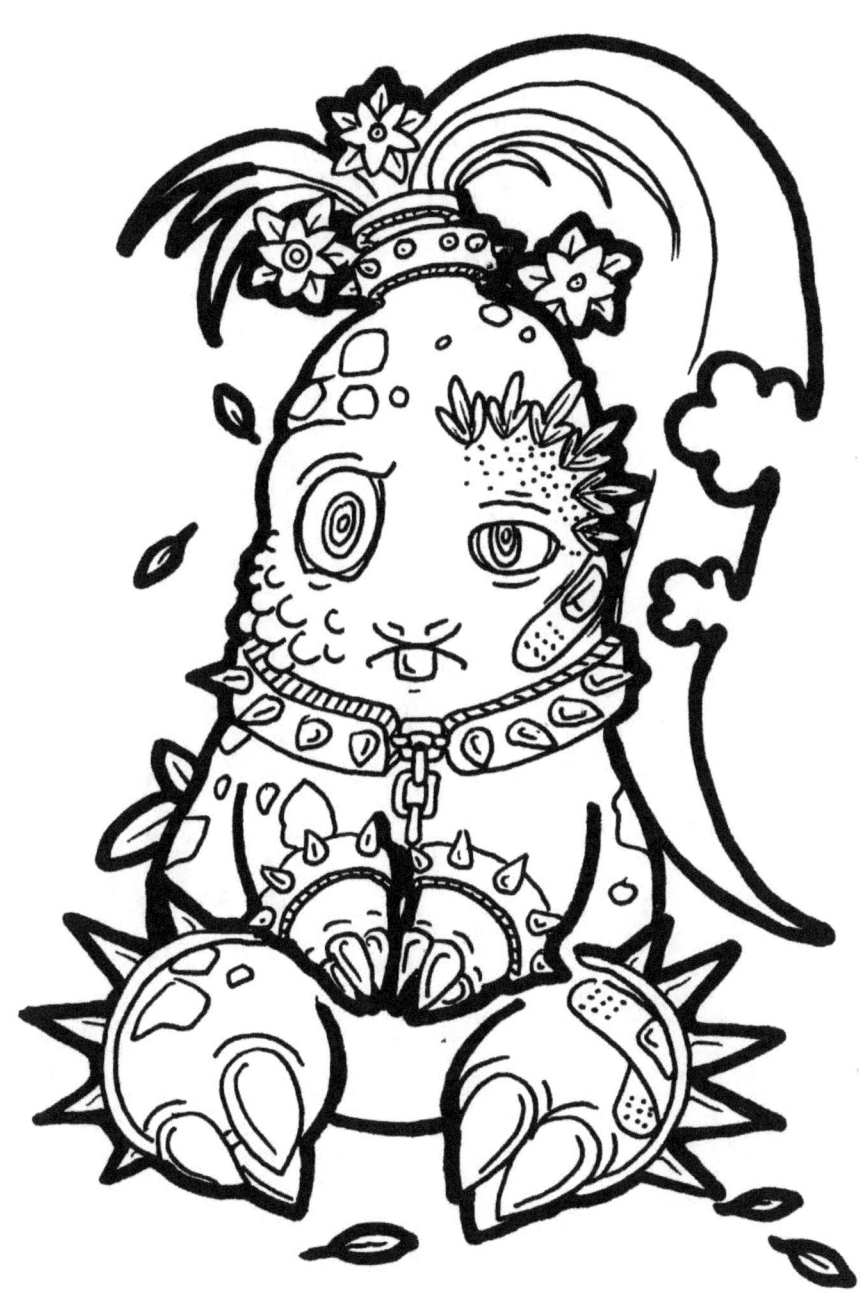

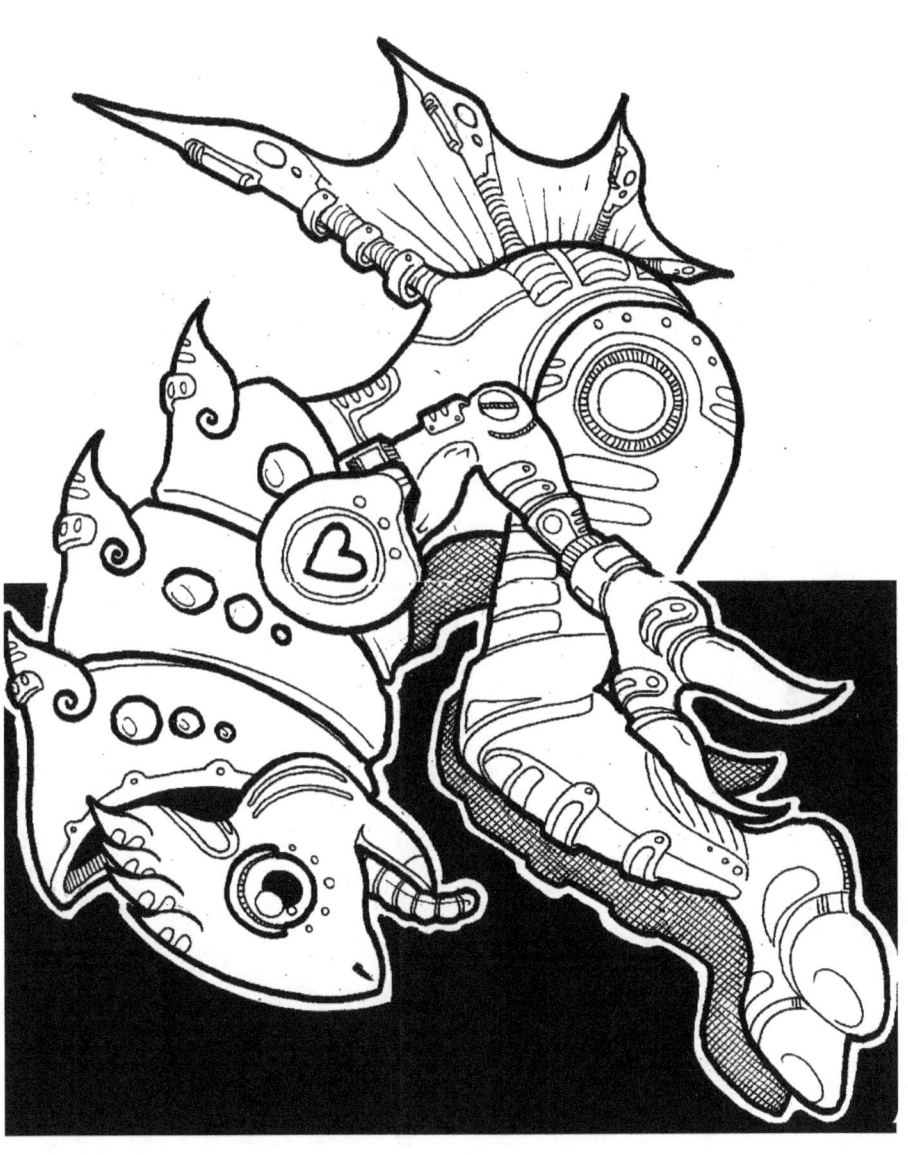

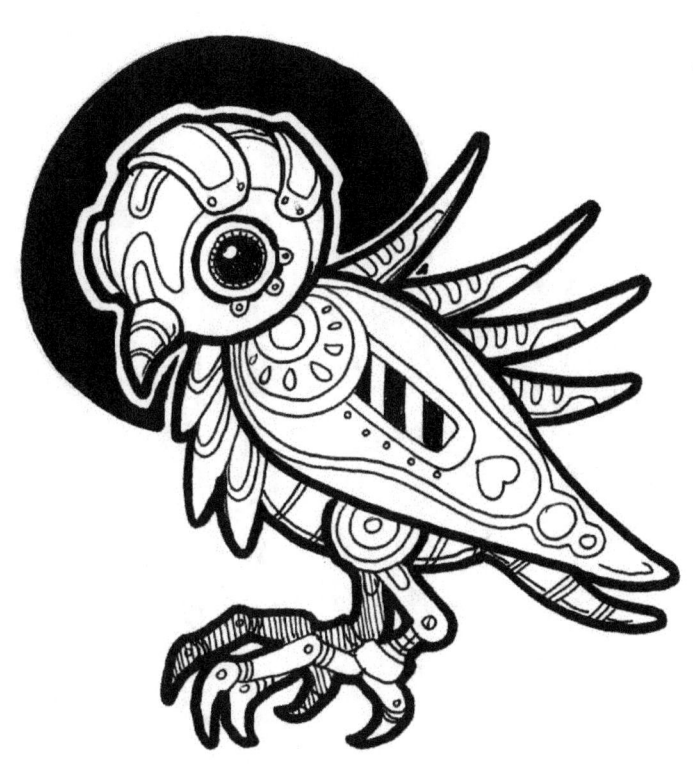

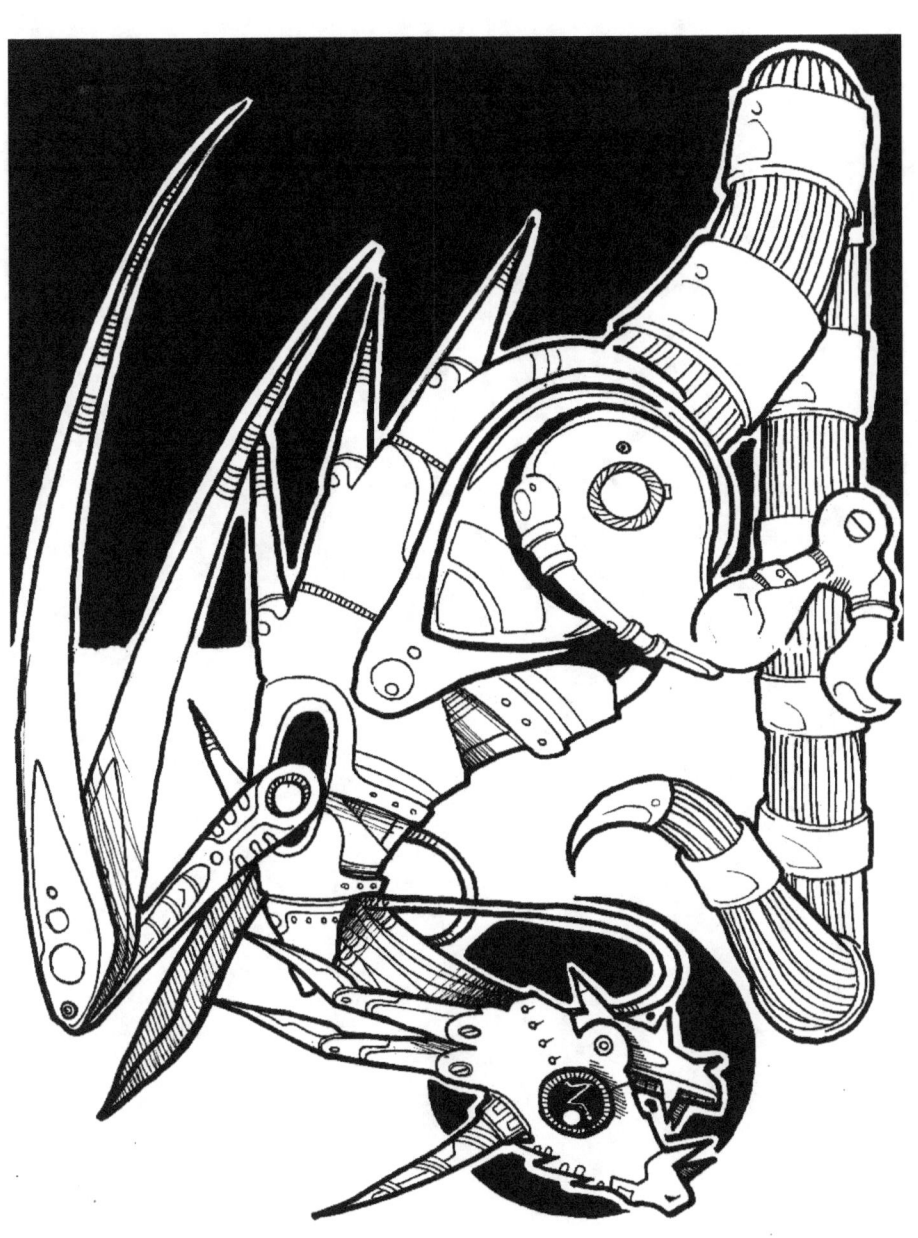

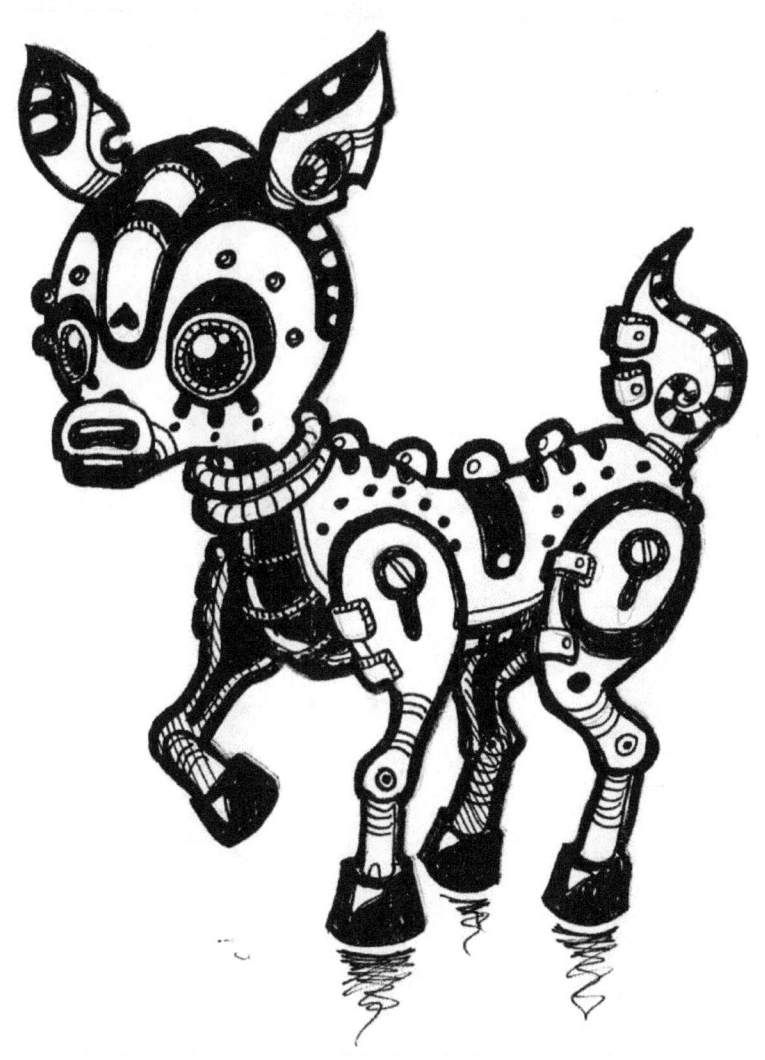

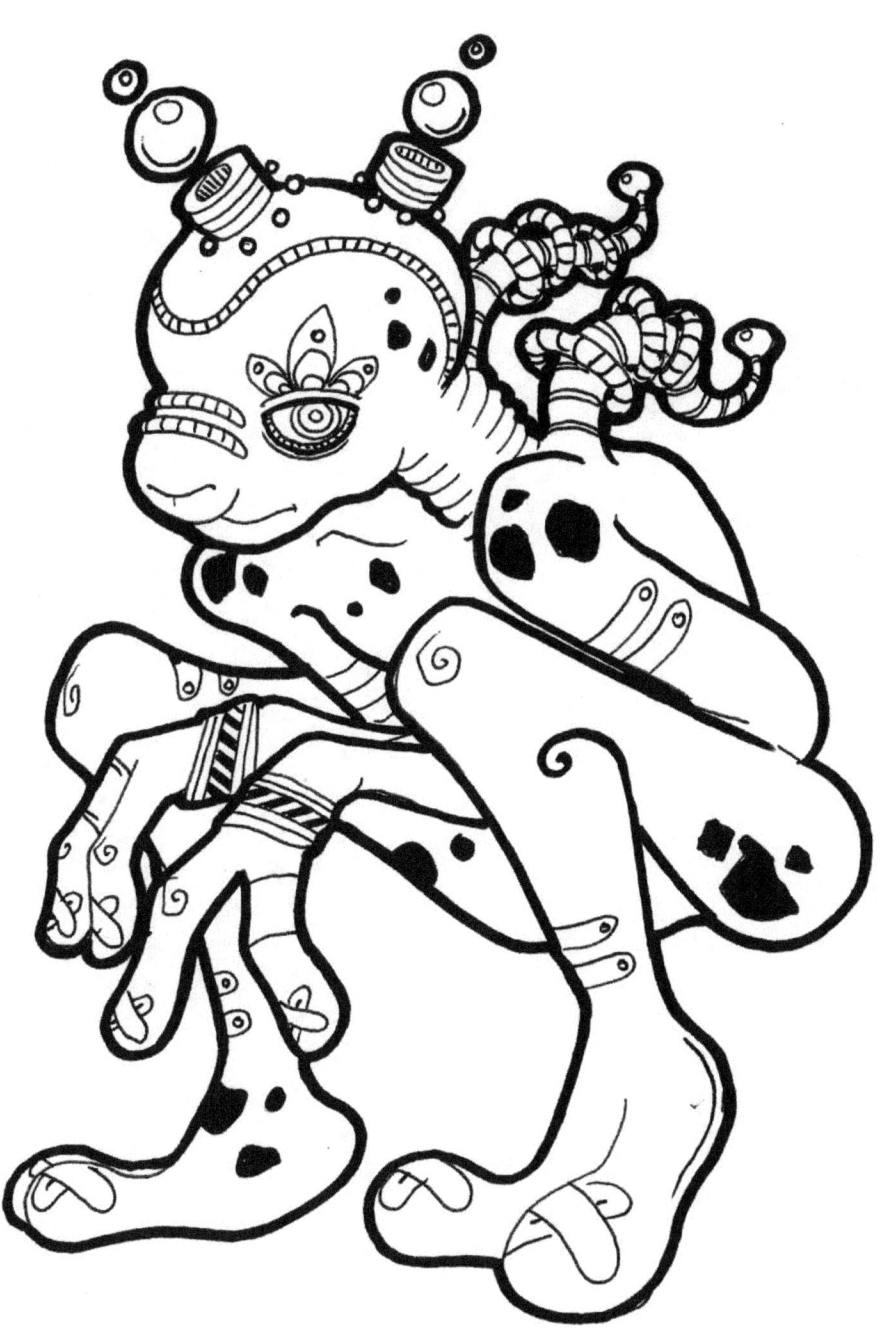

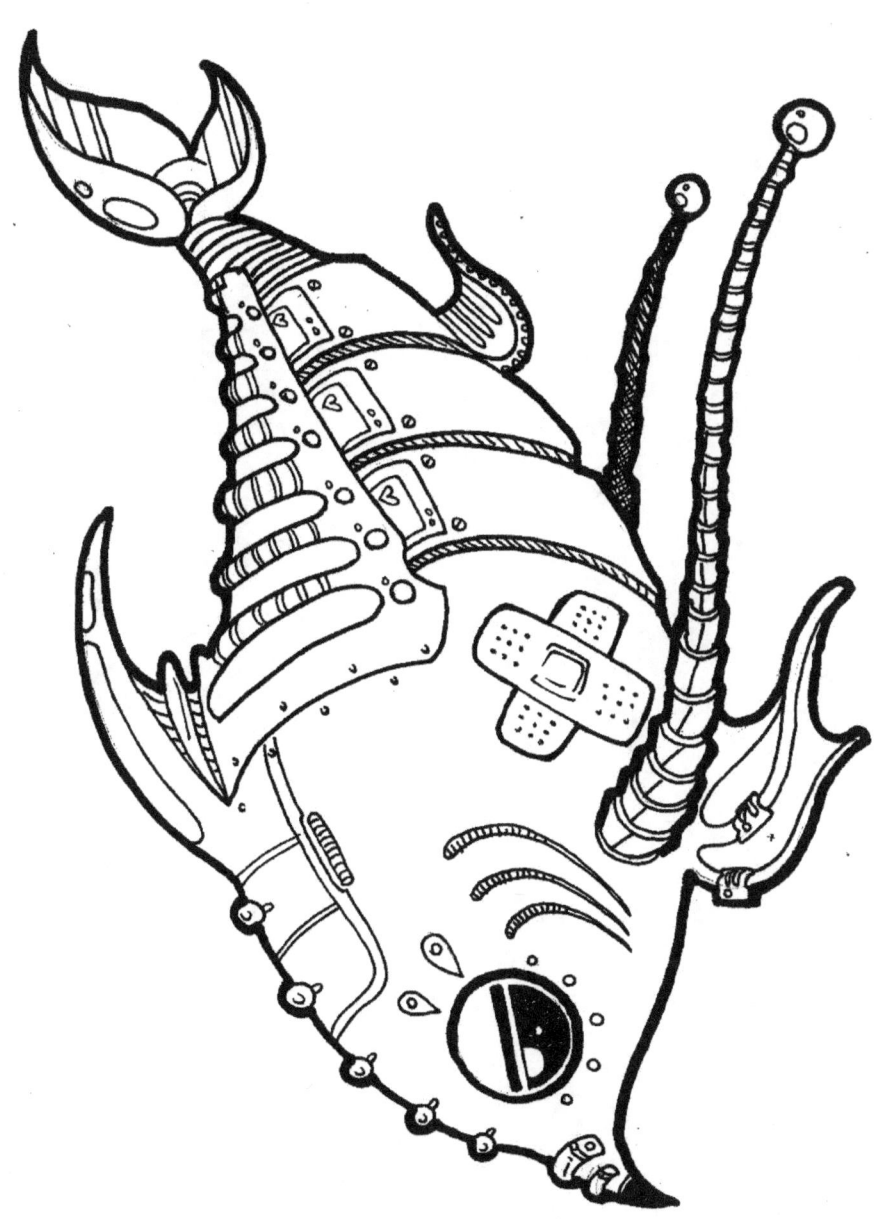

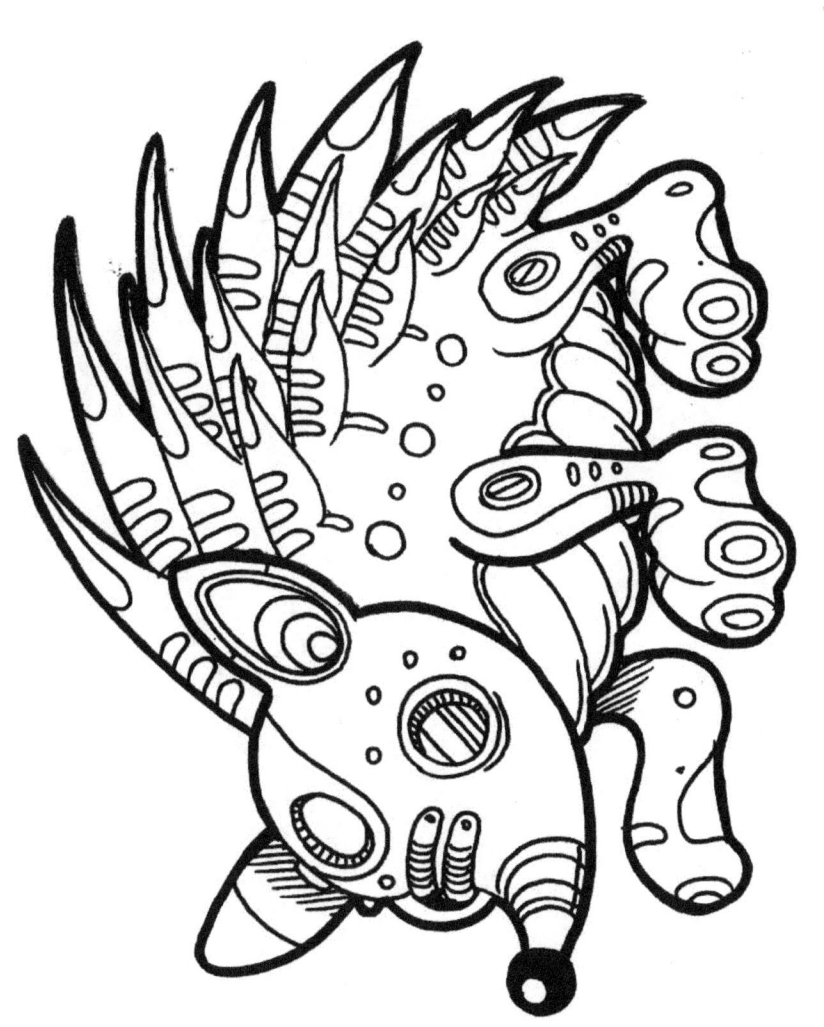

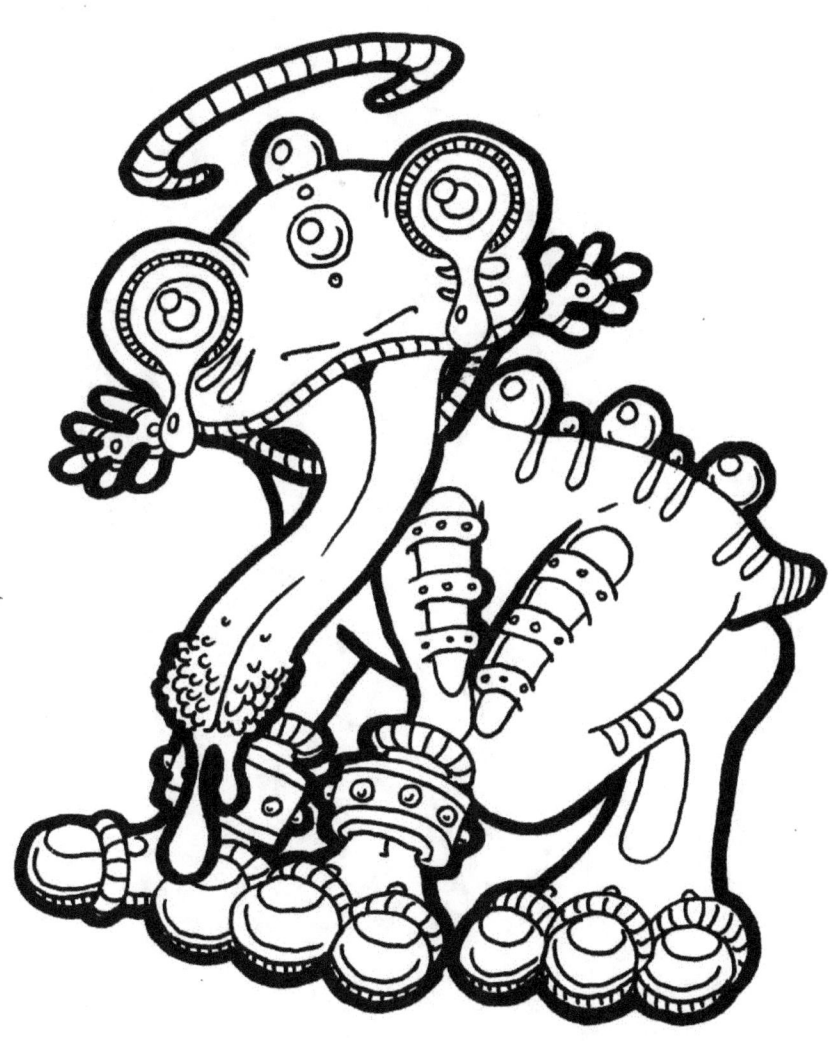

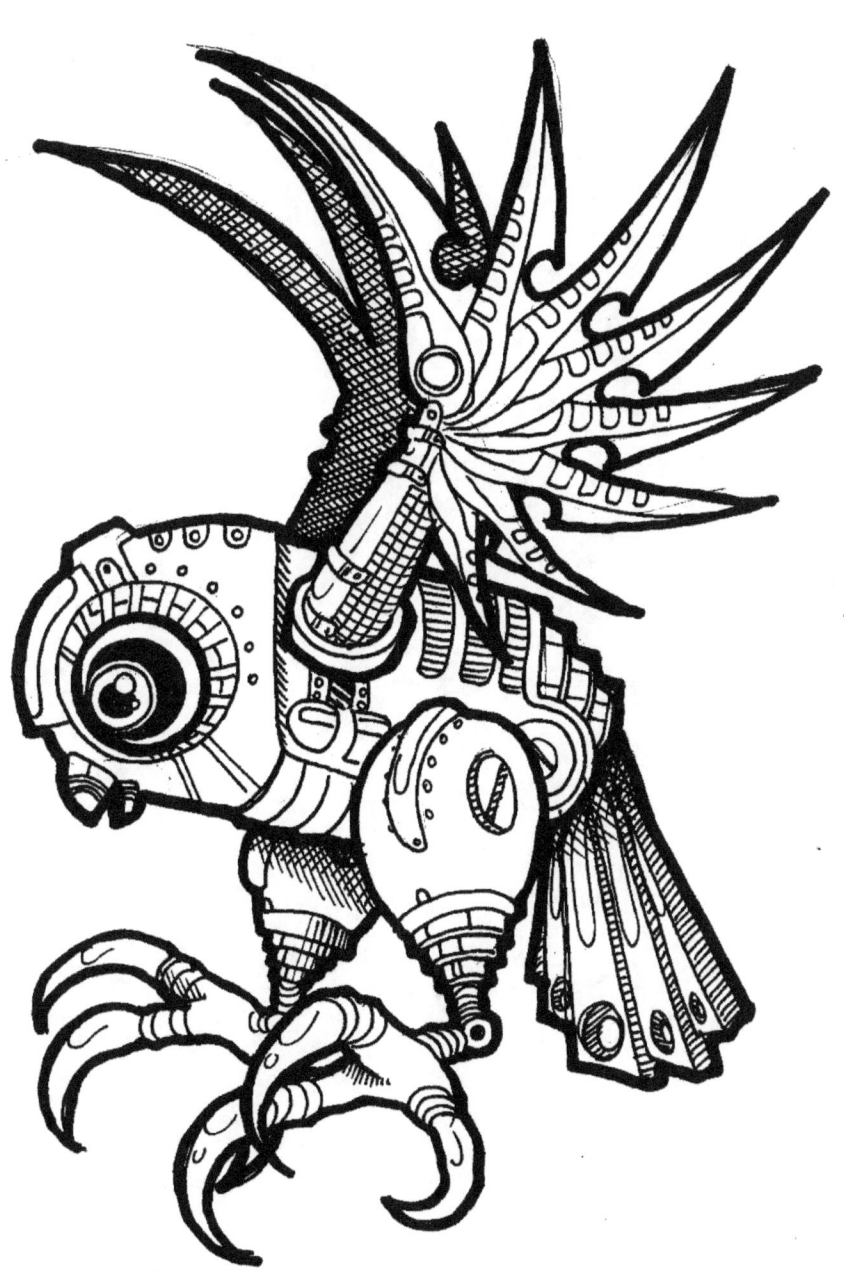

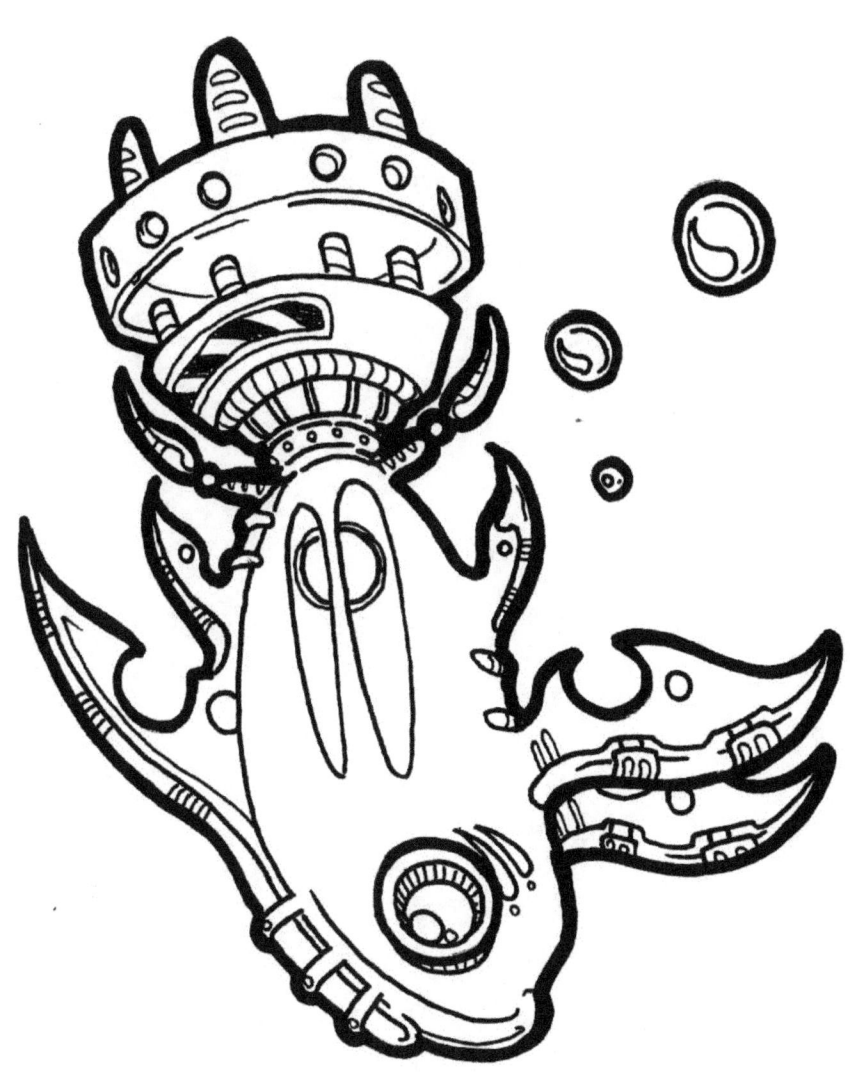

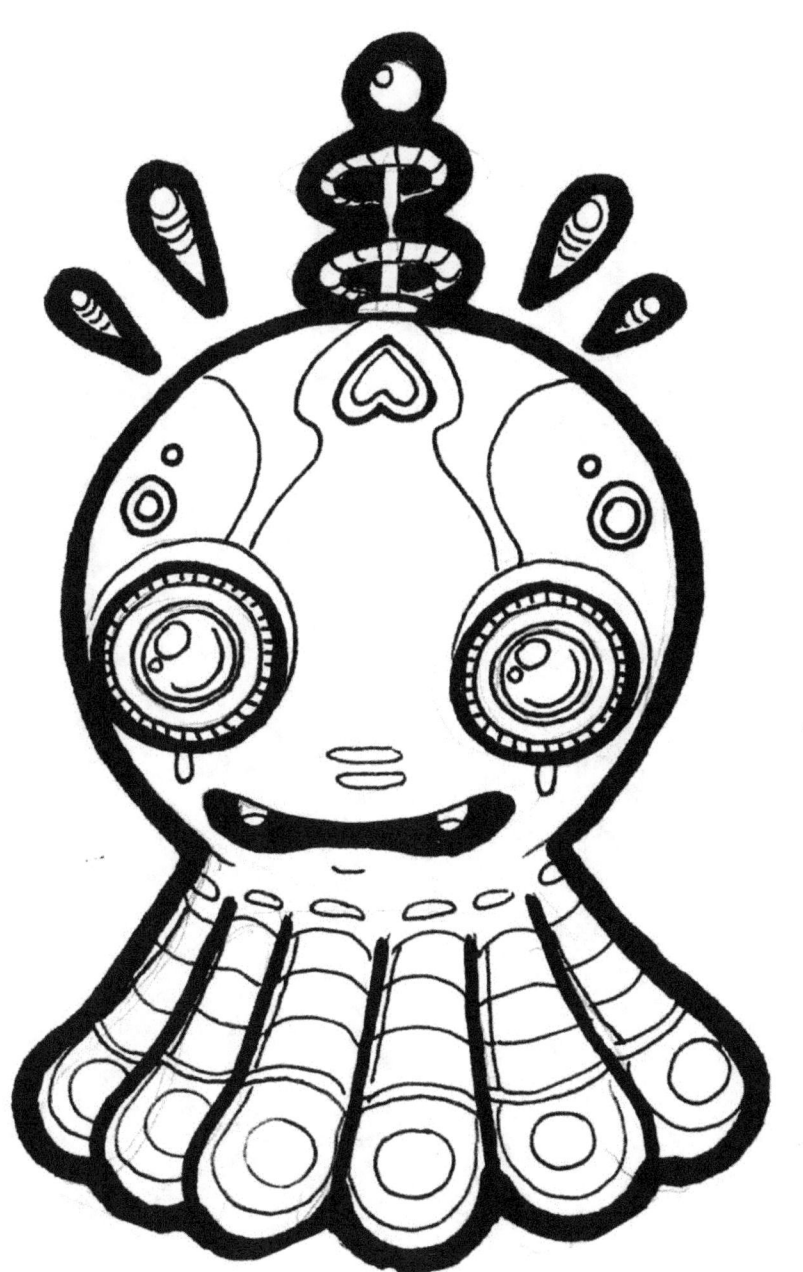

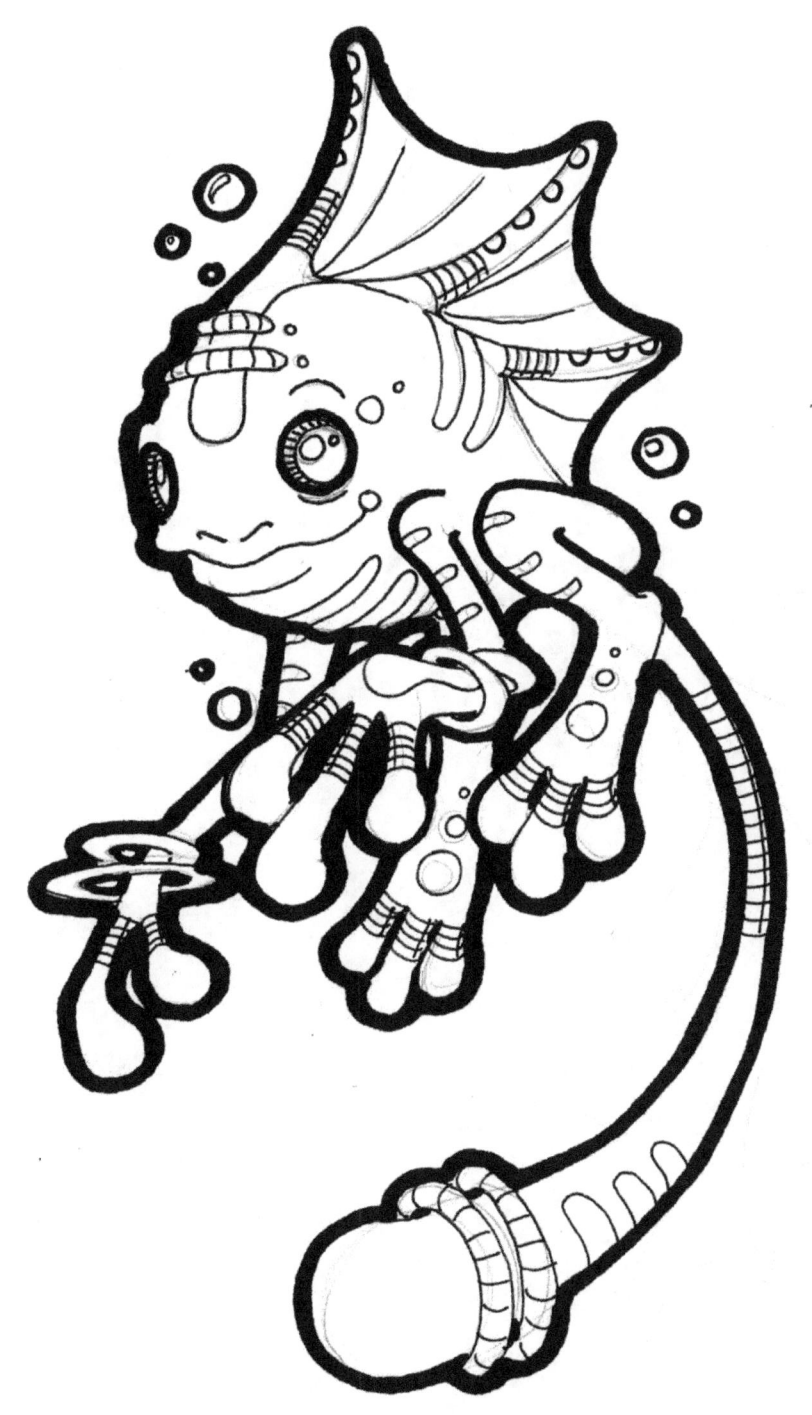

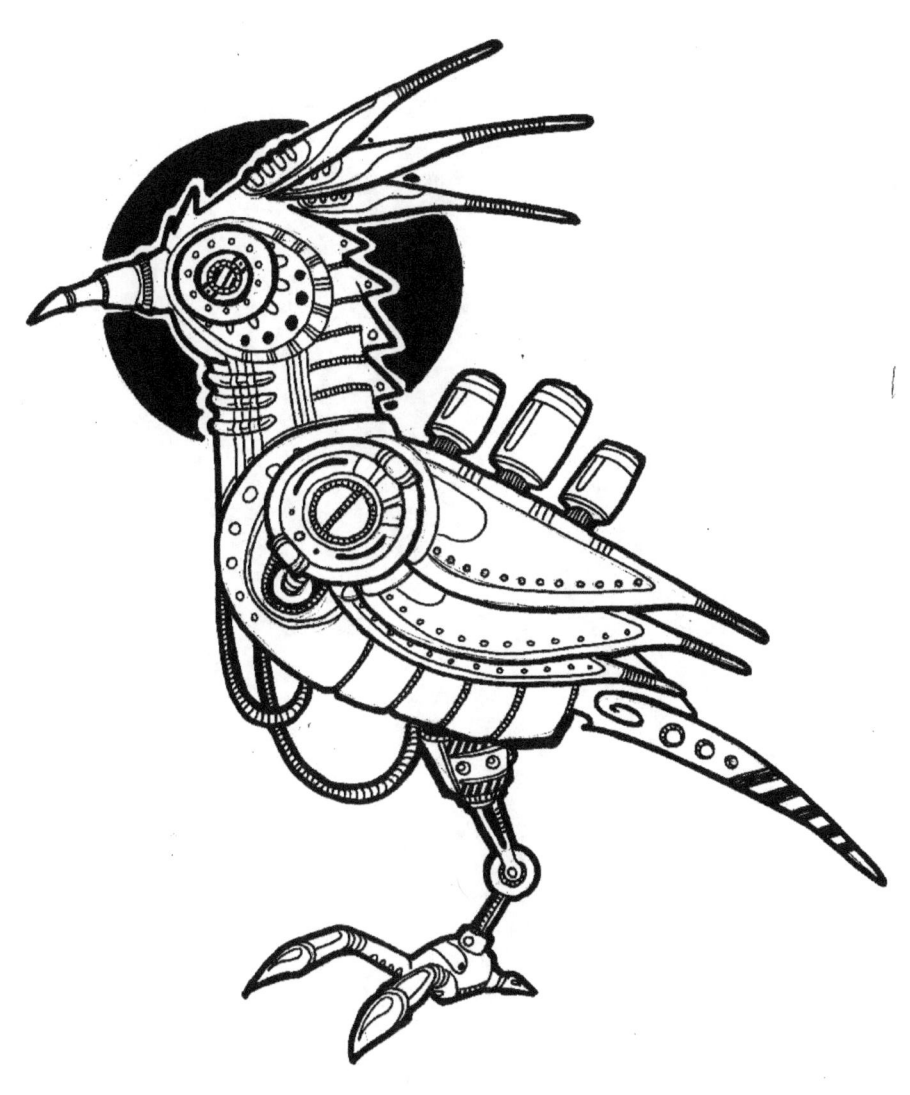

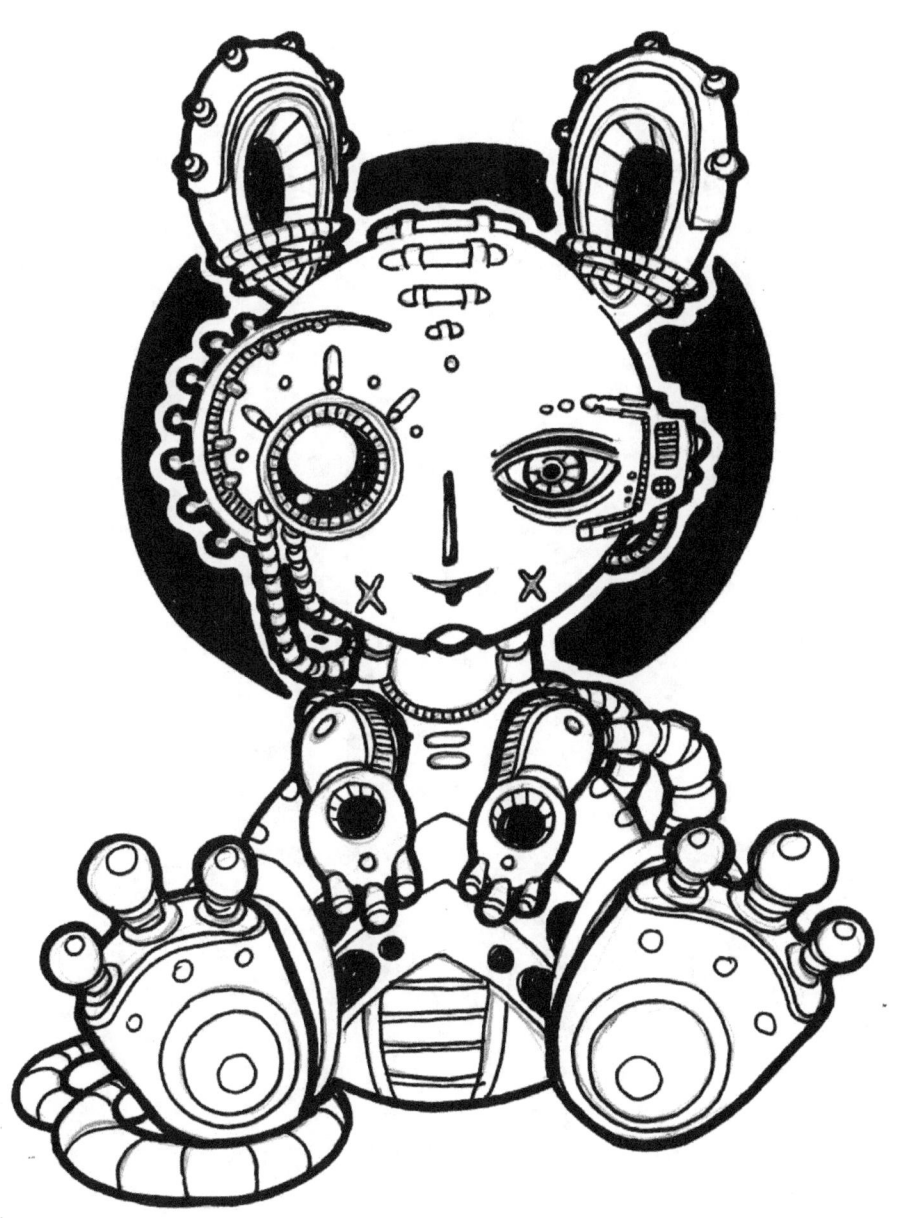

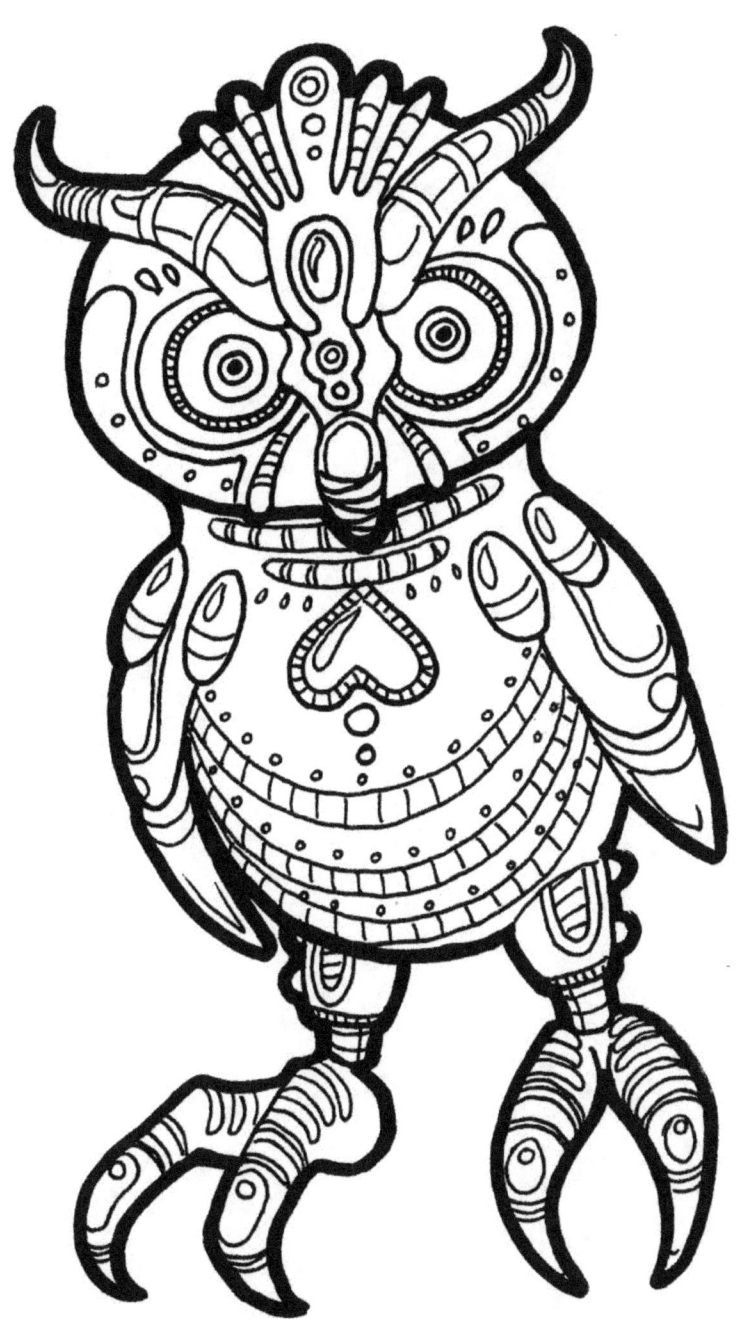

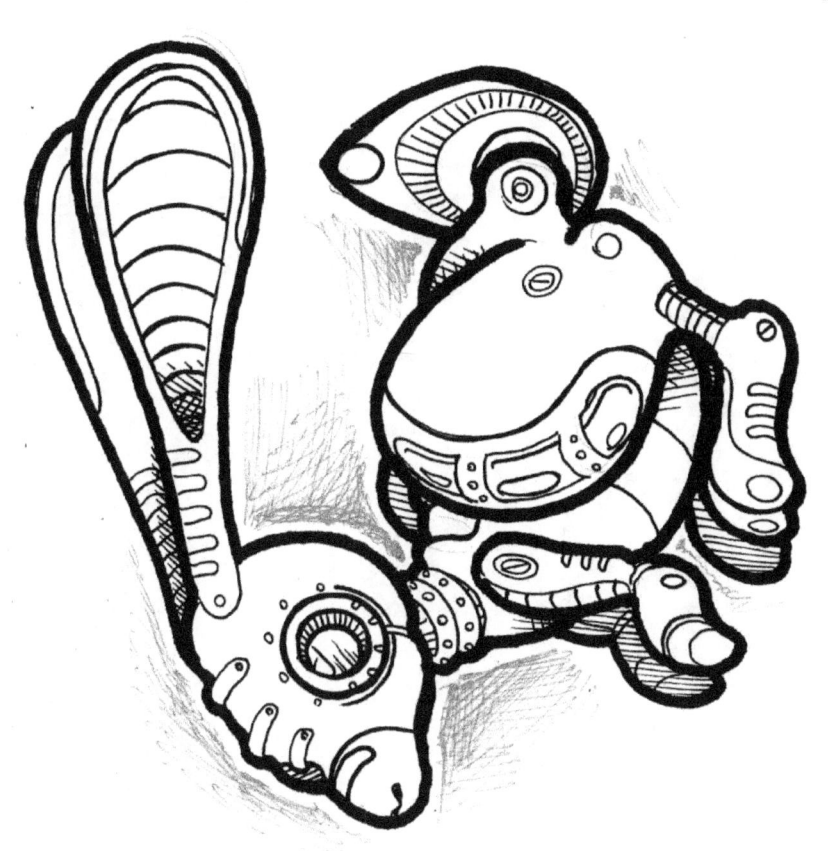

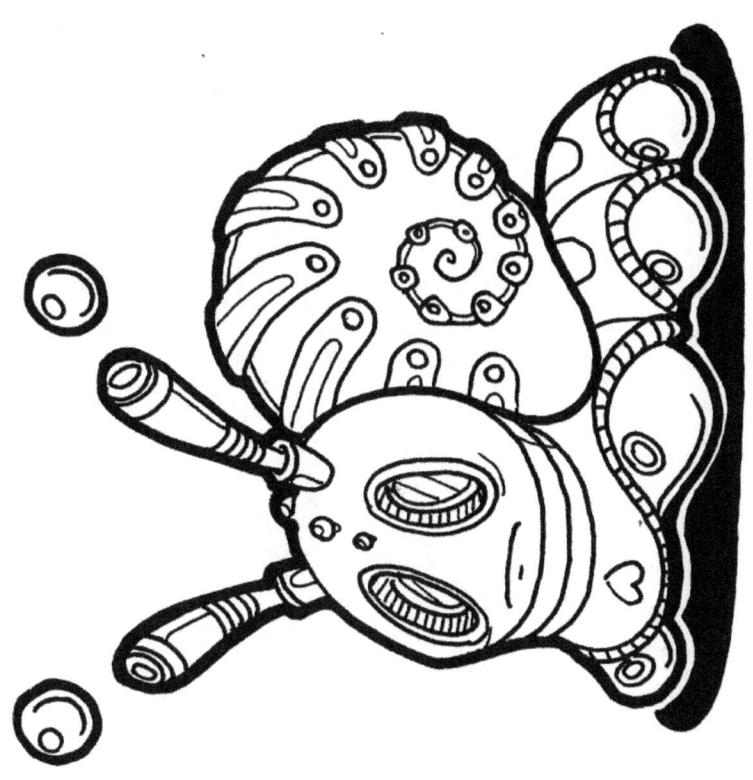

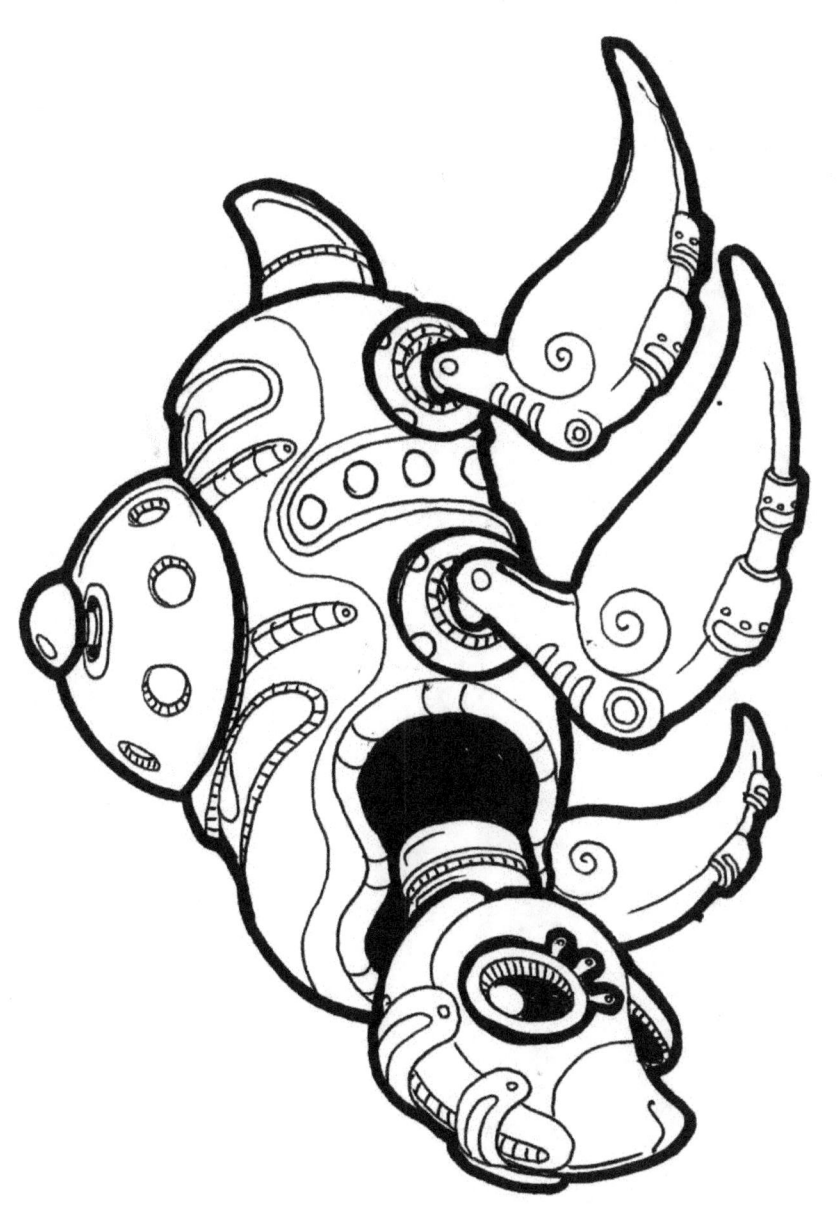

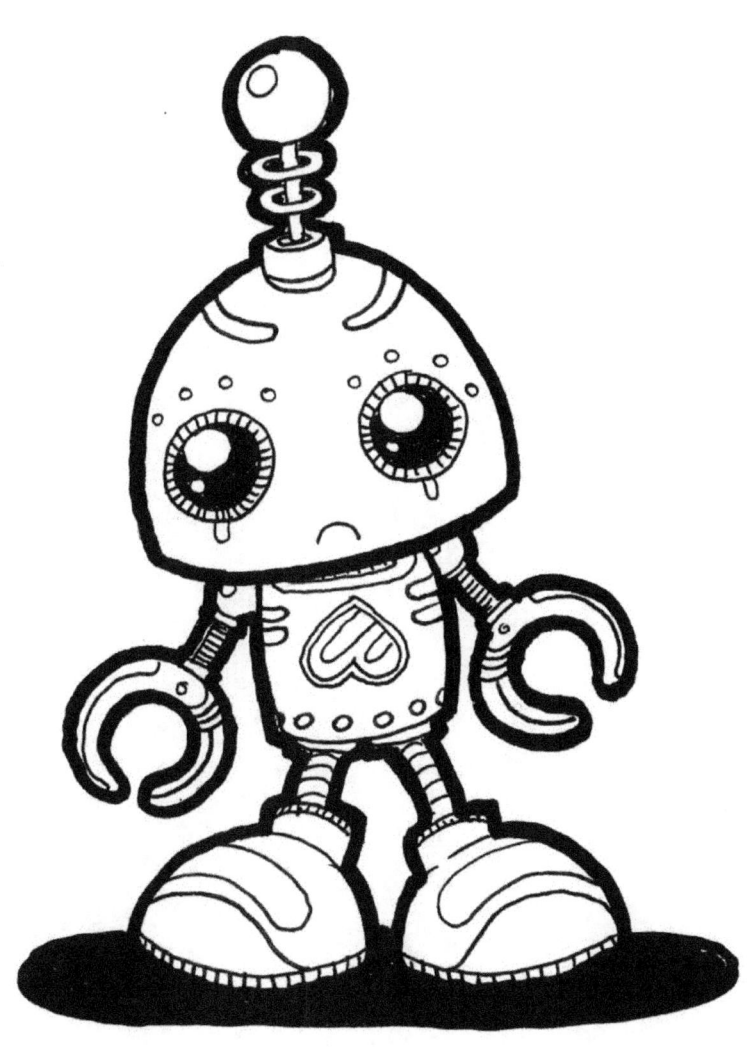

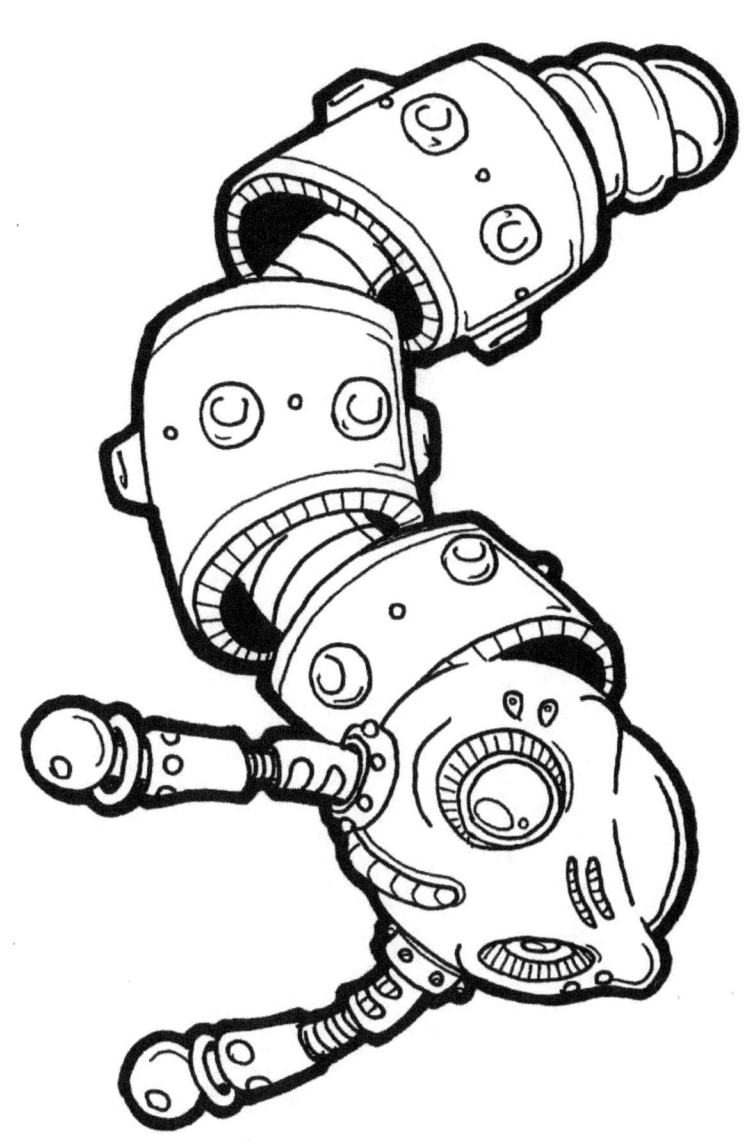